HELEN ALLINGHAM'S
ENGLAND

'ON THE NORTH DOWNS NEAR TITSEY COURT, SURREY'
*is dated May 1876 and was painted soon after Helen's marriage. This
area was easily accessible by rail and the Allinghams made frequent
visits during the late 1870s.*

HELEN ALLINGHAM'S ENGLAND

INA TAYLOR

CAXTON EDITIONS

DEDICATION
For Annabel

This Edition published in 2000 by
Caxton Editions
20 Bloomsbury Street,
London WC1B 3QA
an Imprint of the Caxton Publishing Group

First published by Webb & Bower Ltd in 1990

Text Copyright © 1990 Ina Taylor

British Library Cataloguing-in-Publication Data:
a catalogue record for this book is available
from the British Library

ISBN: 1 84067 087 8

Typeset in Great Britain by P & M Typesetting Ltd, Exeter

Colour reproduction by C S Graphics, Singapore

Printed and bound in Indonesia

HALF-TITLE PAGE:
'COTTAGE AT HASLEMERE':
*Helen said she always counted the rows of tiles on a cottage before she began drawing.
Almost a century later the weather tiles on this house remain the same.*

TITLE PAGE:
*At the time this was painted, the cottage was owned by the Desborough family.
The stream forms the boundary between Surrey and Sussex.*

CONTENTS

INTRODUCTION

A hundred years on, Helen Allingham's images of rural England are enjoying enormous popularity. At one end of the market her paintings fetch ever higher prices while at the other the trade in greetings cards featuring her watercolours is booming. She is most commonly thought of as a painter of cottages but, as the illustrations in this book demonstrate, this was only one facet of her prodigious output. Her work is equally fine when it portrays an intimate domestic scene, the face of a young girl or a family holidaying by the sea. In her lifetime the public wanted nothing but cottage scenes and it is only latterly that the beauty in her other subjects has been appreciated. Recently the pictures painted in her own home, using her children as models, have been the ones making the record prices for an Allingham.

There is much that is modern about Helen Allingham's life and interests. She would not have thought of herself as a feminist and certainly took no part in the suffragette movement, yet from the outset she strove to gain recognition as a professional artist. This was not easy for a nineteenth-century woman to

'A CART BY A VILLAGE INN'
is a glimpse of village life in Shere, Surrey, painted during the Allinghams' summer holiday in 1878. The White Horse Inn was managed by the Askew family for eighty years.

achieve. Whilst many girls were encouraged to learn sketching as a drawing-room accomplishment, it was not deemed appropriate for them to receive proper art training like men. Helen's aunt was the first person to take on the Royal Academy Schools and get them to allow women to become students, and Helen herself became the first female member of the Royal Society of Painters in Watercolours. She asked for no concessions because she was a woman, simply to be able to compete on equal terms with men. By the time she was twenty-two, she had secured a job as the only female working on the *Graphic* magazine. Unusually for a Victorian woman, Helen Allingham worked to support herself and her family for most of her life.

She was just as concerned as we are about the vanishing countryside and its traditions. Her paintings of old Surrey cottages arose in part from a desire to draw people's attention to beautiful old houses which were being destroyed, either by unsympathetic restoration or, worse, by demolition. She was not alone in believing the simple rural way of life to be the best one. Other artists, like her husband's friends amongst the Pre-Raphaelites, celebrated the pastoral life, as did contemporary novelists like Thomas Hardy and George Eliot. At the same time groups of people formed to collect traditional folk songs and dances before they disappeared forever.

The Surrey countryside Helen Allingham made popular in

her art was already a thing of the past. By the last quarter of the nineteenth century it had become a playground for the rich who were quickly conveyed from London by the railway. Summer migrants like Lord Tennyson and George Eliot owned modern country houses, mixed only with their own class and regarded the rustics as a useful pool of labour for house or estate. Very occasionally a local might be paid to pose for one of the increasing number of artists attracted by the beautiful Surrey and Sussex landscape, but usually more healthy-looking professional models were imported from London to grace the paintings.

For the locals, this influx provided a much-needed boost to their failing economy. The agricultural labourer was being forced off the land by machinery and there was a steady exodus to the towns in search of jobs. For those who remained, life was hard. Harvests were not always bountiful. Even when they were, the produce belonged to the landowner who frequently paid his labourer a pittance supplemented by free accommodation in a cottage on the estate. Some of the more artistic landowners liked to keep their cottages as picturesque semi-ruins, similar to the follies erected on other parts of their estates to enhance the view. There was often little regard for the welfare of the family of ten or more clustered into four rooms.

In truth, Helen Allingham's England never really existed. It was always a romantic myth, an escape from encroaching urbanization and technology. However, we would be wrong to criticize her on this account, since her intention was to create a work of art, not an accurate historical record. The early camera was quite capable of reproducing an exact image of the rural scene – and indeed contemporary photographs show a different view from the artist's.

Middle-class Victorians who bought Helen Allingham paintings to hang on their drawing-room walls wanted to escape from reality into an idyllic countryside. Little has changed. Glossy magazines, with fashion models posing in designer 'country clothes' against sun-lit barns, now enjoy a wide circulation. For us, tags like 'old-fashioned' or 'country' appended to advertisements are a recognized shorthand for everything that is good and wholesome. Deep down we know that modern country living is rarely so perfect but, like Helen, we too want to enjoy the beautiful dream.

Although this picture was inspired by an actual scene, Helen used professional models for the figures.

It is unusual to see a young baby in a shawl in an Allingham painting; Helen usually preferred toddlers in her pictures. The detail in 'Beside the Old Church Gate Farm, Smarden, Kent' is so fine, that even the house martin's nest under the eaves is clearly visible.

1

CHILDHOOD AND EARLY ART TRAINING 1848–1866

On 26 September 1848 Helen Allingham was born into a comfortable middle-class family in Swadlincote, Derbyshire.

Her father Alexander Henry Paterson (known as Henry) was twenty-three when his first child Helen Mary Elizabeth was born. He had recently qualified as a surgeon and married nine months earlier. Medicine was not however a profession which ran in the Paterson family, for Henry's father was a Unitarian minister in Stourbridge, Worcestershire, and his mother the daughter of a judge. Although Unitarianism was the most liberal of the nonconformist faiths, it nevertheless exerted a strong influence on Henry and his children. Helen never became a regular attender at chapel in her adult life, but she was strict about the sort of activity she considered permissible on a Sunday: painting was not included, as she told the poet Tennyson firmly when he requested her to complete a picture on the Sabbath.

On her mother's side there was equally strong Unitarian faith, with some members of the Herford family entering the ministry. Helen's mother Mary Chance Herford was slightly older than her husband and the daughter of a Manchester wine merchant. Of more significance is the fact that Helen's mater-

The thatched cottage is Hill Farm, Symondsbury, in Dorset where Helen sometimes went to paint on visits to her Herford relatives.

nal grandmother was an artist. Sarah Smith Herford painted landscapes and portraits in oils so impressively that her work was cited in a publication as late as 1905. It was perhaps this talent which passed to her daughters and granddaughters. Helen's mother and aunts all received art tuition in addition to schooling of an unusually high standard for girls of the time.

Helen's Aunt Laura went on to become a professional artist, settling in London in the artists' quarter around Fitzroy Square. There she had rooms in the same house as the artist-potter William De Morgan who alarmed his fellow lodgers by setting up a kiln in the basement to experiment with new pottery glazes. A few years later Miss Herford's fears were justified when De Morgan's kiln exploded, ripping the roof off the house.

Mary Herford, Helen's mother, shelved her artistic aspirations when she married. Her dowry was used to purchase a medical practice for her husband in Swadlincote, a small village four miles from Burton-on-Trent. The couple took a substantial house in the main street, anticipating that Dr Paterson would build up a thriving clientele in the surrounding country-side. What they did not foresee was the deep suspicion these country folk harboured towards those who were not members of the established church. Paterson's business did not prosper and his wife, ill during pregnancy and childbirth, became

A thatched cottage at Farringford, Isle of Wight, painted during one of Helen's visits to the Tennysons in her later years.

A scene familiar to Helen when she and her husband lived in Surrey: the lane by Witley Church. They walked the area frequently but were not regular churchgoers.

desperately homesick and depressed. She wrote that the village was 'dirty and miserable' whilst its inhabitants were 'very changeable and uncivil'.[1] Within a short time the practice went up for sale.

By the time Helen's first birthday came round she was living in Altrincham, Cheshire, since her father had bought another practice in his wife's home town. This move was successful and the Patersons soon felt sufficiently established to buy land and have a house of their own built on the hills of neighbouring Bowden. This was the area Helen always

This painting of peonies was one of many plant studies Helen made. Usually they were in preparation for a cottage border but this picture is complete in its own right.

associated with the happy years of her childhood. She was surrounded by her Herford relations whose family connections were impressive and included the novelist Mrs Gaskell, descendants of Joseph Priestley the scientist, and prominent Unitarians like the Rylands and Martineaus.

In Cheshire the Paterson family multiplied so that Helen was eventually the eldest of seven children. She was educated at the Unitarian boarding school in Altrincham which her mother had attended and which had originally been set up by Helen's grandmother, Sarah Smith Herford.

Although Helen enjoyed drawing as a child, it was probably the news of her Aunt Laura's victory over the Royal Academy Schools that really determined her to follow an artistic career. Helen was eleven years old when Laura Herford challenged this august establishment to open its doors to women. In 1860 she submitted her artwork signed only with initials, and to her delight received news of its acceptance and a place for A L Herford Esq.

It was unheard of for a woman to attend the country's premier art school, yet Laura demonstrated there was nothing

This faint pencil sketch of Helen's sister Isabel was drawn from a photograph because the little girl had died at the same time as her father from diphtheria.

Henry Walter Paterson, brother of Helen and drawn by her in December 1869. He worked as an agent for a Portuguese wine firm but died at the age of thirty-nine in a lunatic asylum.

in the Academy's constitution specifically forbidding it. Fortunately the Royal Academy's president, Sir Charles Eastlake, was sympathetic to her cause, so she and five other women were admitted and the Royal Academy Schools continued thereafter to accept female students. Laura Herford immediately became Helen's heroine, and her ambition was to follow in her aunt's footsteps. Taking up her pencil, Helen filled her early sketchbooks with drawings of her brothers and sisters, animals she saw around her and places in Wales the

family visited for holidays, as well as illustrations copied from magazines.

When she was thirteen, this carefree childhood came to an abrupt end. In May 1862 a severe diphtheria epidemic broke out in the Bowden area and Dr Paterson soon fell victim to the disease. His attack seemed slight, for just a few days later he was back at work. For three weeks he was out night and day attending his patients. Given the state of nineteenth-century medicine he could do little for the victims except paint their throats with tincture of iron. During the course of such treatment a dying child coughed in his face and, he believed, re-infected him. Although he struggled on seeing patients, he knew his own fate was sealed but hid it from his wife, then heavily pregnant with their seventh child. When he could deceive her no longer, he took to his bed and died after four agonizing days. His son Arthur was born the following month. As everyone watched to see if mother and baby would survive, Helen's three-year-old sister Isabel contracted the disease and died.

Miraculously Mrs Paterson, her baby and the other children escaped infection, but life changed radically for them all. For the teenage Helen it had been a harrowing experience she never forgot. As the eldest, she felt it her duty to take care of the family in whatever way she could, and this strong sense of responsibility for her kin remained with her all her life. To the end of her days and beyond, she provided for her relatives financially, even though some were quite able to support themselves.

Immediately after the funerals of her father and sister, Helen was sent away from the diphtheria epidemic to stay with the Paterson aunts in Birmingham. She was joined later by her surviving brothers and sisters, who had similarly been sent to stay with relations to avoid infection. They were soon reunited with their mother. After the tragedy at Bowden, Mrs Paterson could no longer face living in Cheshire and made her home for the time being amongst her late husband's family in Edgbaston, Birmingham. Although there was much practical help for the family, in terms of education for the girls provided by their Paterson aunts, money was extremely short. Widow and children had to learn the painful lessons of thrift. Once again this early training ingrained itself deeply in Helen. Years later, though a well-known artist able to sell her work for large sums, she remained very careful about money. People observed how she would always collect every discarded scrap of string from a parcel or gather any windfall apples she saw. Others noticed she invariably had an excuse for not being able to donate to charity when asked. But having lived through difficult times as a child, Helen was concerned to conserve as much

One of Helen's illustrations for 'Six to Sixteen', a girls' story by the popular Mrs Ewing. Helen's monogram is in the left-hand corner. She illustrated several of Julia Ewing's stories when working in London (see also page 21).

'EARLY PRIMROSES',
in a wood close to Helen's later home at Sandhills, Surrey . This was a
favourite walk of the family.

of her income as possible lest hard times should strike the family once again.

In Birmingham she continued to show a talent for drawing, which persuaded the Paterson aunts to enroll her at the Birmingham School of Design, then gaining in esteem under the headship of the portrait painter David Wilkie Raimbach. For fifteen shillings a term, Helen was able to study Drawing and Painting, Perspective and Practical Geometry, and Costume, three days a week. It was her intention to work hard and qualify, so that she could obtain an art-teaching post like that held by the Misses Raimbach and Preston who taught her. In order to gain some teaching experience and contribute towards her own schooling, Helen gave art lessons to a younger girl.

At the end of her first year, Helen's single-minded determination won her an honourable mention for drawing the shaded figure, a bronze medal for figure drawing from the cast (plaster copies of classical statues) and, of more significance in view of what was to come, a silver medal for wild flowers drawn from nature. By the end of three years' study, the seventeen-year-old Helen Paterson beat her male counterparts to win the school's Special Prize at the annual prizegiving. This was given for her outstanding anatomical studies (drawn from casts not life). Aware of her potential, Raimbach advised Helen to go to London and seek entry to the Royal Academy Schools, reputed to offer the best art education in the country.

REFERENCES

1 Paterson memoirs (private collection)

OPPOSITE:
'A COTTAGE DOOR':
the young girl watching her kitten was a favourite subject with Helen.

17

2
THE LONDON ART WORLD
1866–1874

Helen arrived in London in the autumn of 1866, having secured a place at the Royal Female School of Art in Queen's Square, Bloomsbury. Here she planned to follow the Advanced Course which would prepare her for admission to the Royal Academy Schools by concentrating on drawing from antique casts.

She found her time spent at the school worth while; writing in the *Graphic* magazine a few years later, Helen said that it was one of the few places where women artists were not only taken seriously, but encouraged. 'It is a great merit of this Female School that it opens a great variety of fields of action to its students, and proffers culture of many kinds. A lady may not be good at portraiture, or book illustrations but she can use her gifts in designing lacework, fans or tiles.'[1]

Since Helen was only eighteen when she came to London, she required chaperoning. It was arranged for her to live in supervised lodgings with other female art students close to the school and for her brief holidays to be spent either in the company of her aunt, Laura Herford, or with another relative,

Helen Paterson's painting of the corner of a house in Verona, executed when she was twenty and about to enter the Royal Academy Schools.

Mrs Eliza Parkes, wife of the wealthy Radical Birmingham MP Joseph Parkes and mother of the feminist campaigner, Bessie Parkes. Both sets of relatives were happy to oversee Helen's welfare and introduce her to some of the leading artists, actors and literary figures in London.

By the summer of 1867, Helen was ready to submit the required chalk anatomy drawing to the Royal Academy. It was accepted and she began the three-month probationary period, attending classes at the Royal Academy Schools in Trafalgar Square from 10am to 3pm every day. Here she had to prepare a set of drawings, appropriately labelled, showing the bones, muscles and tendons of statues set before her. Only when these drawings had been accepted would she receive the all important ivory Ticket of Admission which entitled her to be a student of the Royal Academy. Once again, Helen's work passed on the first submission and she received her Ticket on 8 January 1868. As a reward she was invited by the Parkeses to accompany them on a two-month sketching holiday to Italy.

She returned at Easter, eager to begin the Academy's seven-year training which, she hoped, would transform her into a professional artist. During this long training Helen had to progress from the Antique School to the Preliminary School of Painting and eventually to the Upper School of Painting. Whilst some male students were exempt from the early stages

A pencil sketch of a lady in preparation for drawing on to a wood block for printing.

of the course if they had attended other art courses, women never were because the Royal Academy refused to recognize any qualifications issued by the Royal Female School of Art or similar bodies. As a result, Helen said she had to serve a 'double apprenticeship', the second at a pedestrian pace.

In order to pay for accommodation, she sought work from engraving firms. In the days before photographs could be printed, any pictures required for books or periodicals had to be drawn on to wood blocks by an artist, then cut by an engraver. Most professional artists regarded this as hack work but were often obliged to undertake it in their early days to subsist. Through Laura Herford's friendship with the artist Briton Riviere, Helen secured the necessary letters of introduction to two of the best engravers in London, Harral and Swain. Joseph Swain was impressed by the figure drawings in Helen's portfolio and commissioned her to do four full-page illustrations for the *Once A Week* magazine from July 1868. Since she was new to the work and would probably take longer than a more experienced illustrator he gave her a page a month to produce. This did not yield much money, but Helen was delighted to be following close on the heels of John Millais, Holman Hunt, Frederick Sandys and Frederick Walker in drawing for this popular journal.

Her work was well received and led to commissions to illustrate other periodicals like *Little Folks, Cassell's Magazine* and *London Society.* All this work was executed in between her three days a week at the RA Schools, and she frequently used fellow students as models to avoid the expense of professionals. Money earned from drawing on wood blocks paid for her room in Southampton Street and sometimes left a little to send to her mother. Once Mrs Paterson was sure Helen had settled in London, she moved with her children from Birmingham back to Cheshire where she felt happier among her own family. Although the relatives did assist financially, it was still hard for Mrs Paterson to meet the expenses of a growing family and Helen wanted to help out.

Fortunately it cost nothing to attend the Royal Academy Schools but, as Helen soon realized, this was because there was no real tuition. She progressed easily to the Upper School of

An illustration for a story by Mrs Ewing, drawn by Helen Paterson and engraved by one of the leading London engravers, Harral.

Another of Helen's illustrations for 'Six to Sixteen', serialized in the Aunt Judy Magazine in 1872.

Painting, trusting that when she arrived there she would at last learn something. Instead she became increasingly frustrated. In the Upper School much of her time was spent copying old masters rather than creating her own work. Furthermore, as a woman she was only permitted to draw from draped models, which she felt set her at a disadvantage. And the instruction at this highest level was still haphazard. For one month at a time a 'Visitor' was in charge of the students. He was appointed from the elected members of the Royal Academy and too often regarded the month he was obliged to spend in the Schools simply as a chore. Helen found that the advice meted out by one Visitor was just as likely to be completely contradicted by the following month's Visitor, which left her bewildered. Her desire to paint watercolours was generally scorned by most Visitors who maintained oils were the only medium worth considering. Only the diminutive Frederick Walker, close to her own age and a rising star at the Royal Academy, had any encouragement or advice for her on watercolour technique. During the one month he was the Visitor, she learned more than she had in years, consequently her early work was heavily influenced by his subjects and style.

Dissatisfied with her RA studentship, Helen began taking on more magazine work. Although she cherished a secret hope that she might one day become a 'proper' artist able to spend her days painting the subjects she chose rather than having to do what others dictated, she knew there was small chance of achieving this. Only marriage was likely to remove the need for her to earn a living, and then in all probability a husband would not allow her to pursue her own career or provide her with spare money to send home. Urged on by Laura Herford, Helen set her sights on gaining further work, rather than a husband.

Her work was of a consistently high standard, always met deadlines, and so impressed Joseph Swain that he recommended Miss Paterson to the editor of the *Graphic*. After attending an interview in January 1870, Helen was offered a permanent post on this weekly news magazine, begun only the previous month. William Thomas, editor of the *Graphic*, led the way in producing a periodical which contained more news items than fiction

FASHION REPEATS ITSELF

A detailed drawing by Helen Paterson for a September cover of the Graphic. *She was earning around four hundred pounds a year as an illustrator at this time, which was a lot of money even for a man to earn.*

OPPOSITE:
The composition of 'Gathering Firewood' owes much to the wood-block illustrations for books which Helen had recently undertaken.

Helen sketched this group of ladies, assembled for a dramatic reading at Mr Gladstone's house in Carlton Terrace, for the Graphic. *The Prime Minister is visible at the back.*

and a high proportion of illustrations; that he was prepared to employ a permanent staff, and include one woman amongst them, was quite revolutionary. It also says much for Helen's ability that she gained this sought-after post, since the editor had been a watercolourist and engraver himself. Perhaps resulting from Thomas's own experiences as a commercial artist, he paid excellent rates to those in his employ. Twelve guineas for a full-page illustration and eight for a half-page were some of the highest fees paid to magazine artists at the time, but in return he expected his artists to act as reporters as well.

Although Helen's background had never taught her to pay much attention to fashion, it fell to her as the only woman on the *Graphic* to write the monthly column on what the well-dressed lady around town should be wearing. She was also sent to cover events like flower shows, exhibitions at girls' schools and similar lady-like subjects. Along with sketches she had to submit a report from which copy could be compiled. Other assignments took her to the theatre to review the opening nights of new plays. This was a harder task, since the actors

rarely stood still long enough for them to be drawn, so Helen had to develop her own technique. As her surviving sketch-books show, before the play started and during the interval she concentrated on drawing the set, then during the performance she made lots of lightning sketches of different parts of the actors' costumes. At home she would assemble the complete picture. Alongside her sketches appear pencilled notes about the colours and fabric used which could later be incorporated in her report. The whole experience taught Helen to work quickly, an ability which never left her. A few years later, when painting cottages out of doors, she would get the scene down on paper very fast, then spend a long time finishing it.

Work on the magazine brought her into contact with all manner of people. Frequent visits to the theatre helped introduce her to Tom Taylor, the arts critic and playwright who knew everybody, to Henry Irving who was beginning an outstanding acting career, and to the lively actress Ellen Terry, much the same age as Helen. The friendship between the two women begun in these years lasted a lifetime. In complete contrast to the bohemian set Helen mixed with at Taylor's house in Clapham, her work sent her sometimes into the cream of London society, like that assembled at Mr Gladstone's in Carlton House Terrace. On one occasion, the ladies were gathered to hear dramatic readings by 'the promising young Shakespearean actor, Mr Pennington'. Helen's instructions were to draw the scene and file a report. 'I was placed in the third row from the front,' she wrote in a memorandum to her editor. 'Presently the Princess Louise arrived and everyone rose. In my loyal wish to rise quickly, I spilt all my pencils on the ground, unseen luckily... I could not attend much to the Shakespearean selections, as all energies were devoted to retrieving my pencils and making sketches secretly.'[2] So amused was Mr Thomas by Miss Paterson's excuse for not taking down proper copy that he published her explanation instead.

As she became more established with the *Graphic*, Helen found less time and inclination for attendance at the Royal Academy Schools. Commissions to illustrate books as well as periodicals were also flooding in so that by 1872 she had ceased going to the art school. With another woman artist, she rented a studio and spent her days working as a commercial artist earning substantial sums of money, most of which she despatched to Cheshire. Since she had not given up the idea of eventually becoming a painter, Helen enrolled for evening classes at the newly founded Slade School which, under the direction of Edward Poynter, was leading the way in offering equal opportunities to male and female artists. Working alongside Kate Greenaway, also to become a good friend, Helen was at last able to tackle life-drawing. In the odd moments she had

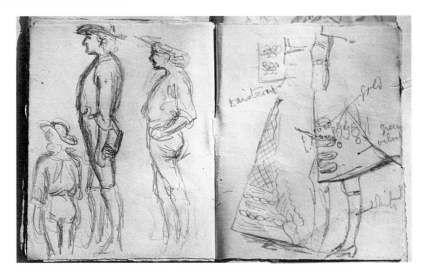

ABOVE RIGHT:
This handmade sketchbook, only about three inches high, was used by Helen to make discreet sketches of the play The Wandering Heir *as it was performed at the Prince of Wales' Theatre in 1874. From these notes she compiled her illustration for the* Graphic.

RIGHT:
Helen Paterson in her early twenties at the time she worked as an illustrator-cum-reporter on the Graphic.

*Helen called this picture 'Japonica' after the brilliantly coloured shrub
by the door. It was exhibited in 1885.*

OPPOSITE:
*One of Helen Allingham's earlier paintings where the large central
figure shows the influence of Frederick Walker.*

left, she returned to her watercolours and began painting subjects of her own choice – noticeably influenced by the paintings Frederick Walker was exhibiting.

The early 1870s were satisfying years for her, since she was able to follow the career she wanted and help support her family by it. It was an especial pleasure for her to be able to finance the art training of her favourite sister Caroline, eight years her junior and already set to follow in Helen's footsteps. The only shadows on the horizon at this time were two unexpected deaths. In October 1870, she was fetched from her lodgings by an agitated William De Morgan who, concerned by the non-appearance of his fellow lodger in Fitzroy Square, had broken the door down. Inside the room, he had discovered the body of Laura Herford. She had died from an accidental overdose of chloroform taken for toothache. She was thirty-nine and, after the acceptance of six paintings by the Royal Academy, was believed to have a promising career ahead of her.

Equally unexpected and even more harrowing was the summons to return home immediately, which Helen received in November the following year. In Cheshire, she found her seventeen-year-old sister Louisa rapidly wasting away from consumption (tuberculosis). There was little Helen could do but stay with her family until the end and share the nursing with her mother. During the hours she sat with Louisa, Helen made several pencil sketches of her sister and one very beautiful but poignant little watercolour.

When she returned to London in the new year, Helen threw herself into her illustrating work. One prestigious commission which came to her was to supply drawings for Thomas Hardy's new novel *Far From the Madding Crowd* to be serialized in *Cornhill*. Work for the *Cornhill* brought her into the company of its editor Leslie Stephen and his sister-in-law Annie Thackeray, daughter of the novelist. The independent twenty-five-year-old Miss Paterson was popular and the

A self-portrait by Caroline Paterson, Helen's sister, who also trained as an artist and whose portrait work is virtually indistinguishable from her more famous sister's.

OPPOSITE:
Helen returned home to assist with the nursing of her sister Louisa, suffering from a terminal spinal disease. This gentle study was made a few days before Louisa's death on 15 November 1871.

frequent recipient of invitations to dine with them and others in that circle. Thomas Hardy, though engaged to Emma Gifford at the time, dined with Helen and Annie Thackeray on occasion during May 1874 and was smitten by his attractive illustrator. Although nothing came of the encounter, years later when Hardy was unhappy in his own marriage, he liked to muse on what might have been if things had worked out differently and he wrote a four-stanza poem entitled 'The Opportunity (For H.P.)':

> *Forty Springs back, I recall,*
> *We met at this phase of the Maytime:*
> *We might have clung close through all,*
> *But we parted when died that daytime.*
>
> *We parted with smallest regret;*
> *Perhaps should have cared but slightly,*
> *Just then, if we never met:*
> *Strange, strange that we lived so lightly!*
>
> *Had we mused a little space*
> *At that critical date in the Maytime,*
> *One life had been ours, one place,*
> *Perhaps, till our long cold claytime.*
>
> *– This is a better thing*
> *For thee, O man! what ails it?*
> *The tide of chance may bring*
> *Its offer; but nought avails it!*

Although Hardy believed marriage might have resulted from the meeting, he was wrong. Helen had already met a much older poet who like herself was fond of the theatre and a great friend of the critic Tom Taylor. In June 1874 Helen Paterson announced her engagement to William Allingham.

REFERENCES

1 *Graphic* 13 Jan 1872 p39
2 *Graphic* 18 May 1872 p455

3
MARRIAGE AND PAINTING
1874–1881

There was surprise in the Paterson family that twenty-five-year-old Helen should have fallen in love with someone double her age. Indeed, at fifty, William Allingham was even slightly older than Mrs Paterson. After meeting him, however, their reservations vanished and arrangements for the wedding went ahead immediately.

As William Allingham wrote to Tennyson's wife at the beginning of August 1874: 'I am to be married! On the 22nd! The lady is Miss Helen Paterson, an artist of some reputation, two of her drawings were in this year's Royal Academy and she has drawn many woodcuts for the "Cornhill" and "Graphic". She is a full score of years my junior, which is to be regretted; but as she and her mother declare that IN THIS PARTICULAR CASE, it is an advantage, and nobody else objects (in fact our intention is as monotonously approved as that of Lydia Languish and her lover) we must make the best of it. I have taken a house in this neighbourhood. I have also taken Helen to Carlyle, who is highly satisfied –. She is especially pleased at the prospect of going on with her art, not only without

Helen's favourite portrait of her husband William which she painted a few months after their marriage when he was fifty. A copy of this picture hangs in the Dublin Portrait Gallery.

hindrance, but with every encouragement from her husband. We have a great many friends in common and trust under Heaven to be in everyway good to each other and to keep our friends.'[1] The marriage did indeed turn out just as happy and successful as they hoped.

William was originally from Ballyshannon, County Donegal, and had worked for the Irish Customs and Excise for some twenty years. This had not been his choice. He had really wanted a literary career but was obliged to leave school and enter first banking, then Customs work, when his father became ill. To console himself, Allingham had struck up a correspondence with many leading literary figures, like Leigh Hunt, Tennyson and Browning, and began writing poetry himself. In the 1850s he arrived in London to try his luck as a journalist but returned home disillusioned after a couple of years. During his time in the English capital though, he made many friends, notably among members of the Pre-Raphaelite brotherhood. It is Allingham who is reputed to have discovered the 'Stunner' Lizzie Siddal (later to be Rossetti's wife) working in a hat shop.

Because London seemed to Allingham to be the cultural centre, he arranged to transfer to the Customs there in 1862 but, following a broken engagement to Alice Macdonald (sister to Georgie Burne-Jones and later mother of Rudyard Kipling),

The new Mrs William Allingham, in a fashionable studio portrait to celebrate her marriage in August 1874.

he transferred again to a post at Lymington in Hampshire. With Tennyson living on the opposite side of the water, on the Isle of Wight, Allingham renewed his early acquaintance and continued writing and publishing his own poetry. One of Allingham's long poems appeared in twelve instalments in *Fraser's Magazine*, and this began a working relationship with the magazine which led to him being offered the post of sub-editor in 1870.

Since William Allingham and Helen Paterson were both involved in journalism, their paths sometimes crossed. Both were fond of the theatre, friendly with Tom Taylor and regularly to be found at his soirées. William's intimacy with the Pre-Raphaelites also brought him into contact with artists such as William De Morgan and Briton Riviere, also friends of Helen's. Possibly it was the loss of her father so early in her teens which drew Helen to the gentle Irish poet, old enough to be her parent. Although they had moved in similar circles for several years, there was no romantic involvement between them until 1874, when William was offered the editorship of *Fraser's*. With a salary of four hundred pounds a year, he felt able to propose marriage to Miss Paterson.

Helen was a convinced Unitarian, so the marriage took place at the chapel at Little Portland Place on 22 August 1874. Appropriately enough for two who worked in journalism, the service was conducted by Peter Clayden, leader writer and assistant editor of the *Daily News* as well as a preacher at the Free Christian Church, Kentish Town.

The letters and gifts the newlyweds received came from impressive sources: Burne-Jones sent his congratulations and reminded William there was a painting awaiting his collection; Barbara Bodichon wrote to say she had put three pictures and various pieces of Arabian furniture aside for them; Robert Browning and his sister sent their warmest congratulations; Tennyson gave the couple a red morocco leather edition of his *Queen Mary* poems, whilst Carlyle and his niece wrote to say they were experiencing difficulties delivering the crates of Apollinaris Water to the Allinghams. (This newly discovered aerated mineral water was enjoying a vogue out of all proportion to its actual worth, many believing the beverage to be equal to champagne.) This was the sort of company the new Mrs Allingham would keep.

It was the words and presence of Thomas Carlyle which dominated the early years of the Allingham marriage. The octogenarian philosopher lived in Cheyne Row, Chelsea, and William had made a special point of taking his fiancée there to be vetted after he had proposed marriage. So greatly did Allingham venerate Carlyle that it is quite likely that if the sage had taken a dislike to Miss Paterson the wedding would have been called off. Fortunately Carlyle approved. The house William leased for his bride was in Trafalgar Square, Chelsea (since renamed Chelsea Square), only a couple of streets from Cheyne Row, thus enabling the Allinghams to be virtually daily callers at Carlyle's. It was not easy for Helen to adjust to the continual company of the elderly dour Scot but luckily for her Mary Aitken was living at Cheyne Row. She was Carlyle's niece and had been brought down to London to take charge of the great man's house following the death of his wife. The two women became lifelong friends.

Wherever Helen went she took her sketchpad and was in the habit of quietly pencilling away. However, Carlyle immediately protested: 'I'll have nothing to do with any sketching.' Helen was not easily put off and continued making drawings of him. One of him sitting reading in the garden, with his cat Tibbs and his long clay pipe on the ground alongside him, met with the complaint that Mrs Allingham made him 'look like an old fool'. Helen also came in for criticism from her husband's friend, the art critic John Ruskin, who said she had portrayed Carlyle as a lamb instead of the lion he really was. She was unperturbed. Carlyle was not the easiest of subjects, suspicious of her drawing and refusing to look in her direction, but gradually Helen won him round by explaining that she did not want him to pose, merely to carry on as normal. The results of her efforts are some dozen watercolours and many pencil sketches showing informal studies of the philosopher towards the end of his life. The portraits finally met with Carlyle's approval; he grudgingly admitted that Mrs Allingham did have a talent for portraiture, which was the only form of artwork he recognized.

Marriage meant that Helen had to give up her post on the

The interior of Limpsfield Church, Surrey, in 1870 showing the box pews. Helen exhibited a watercolour of the church the following year at the Dudley Gallery, Piccadilly.

Graphic. It would not have been seemly for a lady to continue working for a magazine after her marriage. She was not disappointed as she had worked four years for the paper and been able to give a great deal of financial help to her mother. It had been a valuable experience but the quantity of work involved severely curtailed the painting she really wanted to do. In 1870 Helen had begun exhibiting some chalk and line drawings at the Dudley Gallery in Piccadilly and she continued to show her work every year thereafter, progressing on to watercolours. Some of the subjects were based on illustrations she had originally supplied for the *Graphic*, whilst others were predominantly figurative in the style of Frederick Walker. The real highlight of her artistic career came shortly before her marriage in 1874 when two of her paintings, 'The Milkmaid' and 'Wait For Me', were accepted for the Royal Academy Summer Exhibition. To her delight, they also sold during the exhibition. Her success at the RA brought in commissions for further

The interior of Carlyle's dining room at Cheyne Row, a couple of streets from the
Allinghams' house, painted in February 1881.

*The Allinghams were regular visitors to Thomas Carlyle's home in London and Helen made
several drawings of the great man. The background detail in this and her other pictures
of the house has been of value to the National Trust in their restoration work.*

THE TINSMITHS' SHOP.

See p. 42.

*Helen's original illustration for 'A Flat Iron For A Farthing'; this she
later worked up into the watercolour which gained her admission to the
Royal Society of Painters in Watercolours in 1875.*

paintings. It was one of these, 'A Flat Iron For A Farthing', the reworking of a former book illustration, that William Allingham showed to his friend, the eminent watercolourist Alfred Hunt. So impressed was Hunt by Helen's abilities that he offered to assist her election to the Royal Society of Painters in Watercolours. He went through her portfolio and selected the pictures he thought best displayed her talent, then personally undertook to propose her election. In 1875 Helen Allingham achieved the rare honour for a woman of becoming an Associate of the Royal Watercolour Society. Women were not admitted to full membership until 1890, at which time she was immediately elected.

Although Helen gave up her post on the *Graphic*, she did continue with some freelance work after her marriage, providing illustrations for Annie Thackeray's story 'Miss Angel', serialized in the *Cornhill*, and for several minor books of stories and poems for girls. She did, however, decline personal requests from George Eliot, Thomas Hardy and Tennyson to illustrate their latest writings. After 1877 Helen preferred to recommend her sister Caroline Paterson for commissions, since Caroline had successfully completed her art training and made a home in London with her mother and brother Arthur.

Marriage brought children for Helen, but this did not hinder her art career. She was still calling at Cheyne Row to complete a portrait of Carlyle three days before the birth of her first child. Her son, christened Gerald Carlyle in honour of the sage, was born in November 1875 and was followed in February 1877 by a daughter Eva Margaret, always known as Evey. Whilst Helen enjoyed her two children, they nevertheless spent most of their time with a nursemaid. Only the birth in 1882 of her third child, Henry William, whom she adored, made any difference to her life. The silver locket she wore contained only his photograph and lock of blond hair.

OPPOSITE, RIGHT:
'THIS YEAR, NEXT YEAR, SOMETIME, NEVER'
was given by Queen Mary to the Superintendent of Governesses at Petersham Lodge, Surrey, in gratitude for her services during the 1930s.

A rare cartoon by Helen Allingham to illustrate a humorous poem by her husband; both were included in their joint 1885 production Rhymes for the Young Folk.

Helen still had the freedom to spend her days painting. In the seven years the Allinghams lived in London, she exhibited over one hundred watercolours, predominantly at the winter and summer exhibitions of the Royal Society of Painters in Watercolours in Pall Mall. Apart from a few portraits of her husband and Carlyle, Helen's work tended to feature one or two major figures in a landscape, much as Walker's had done. The scenes were frequently rural and often inspired by family summer holidays. Although she did her sketching out of doors, the painting was carried out in her studio where she could also pose her models.

Initially summers were spent by the sea at Eastbourne or Margate which provided her with a different backdrop, then in 1878 the Allinghams rented a cottage in Surrey. From May when the woods were carpeted with bluebells until late September when autumn colours were in evidence, the Allinghams and their two children stayed at Shere near Guildford. Although out of London, William was still able to

This seaside scene, 'Near Beachy Head', painted during the Allinghams' summer holiday, is packed with interest.

These women haymaking were painted in the late 1870s and demonstrate Helen's transition from large central figures to smaller figures in a landscape.

'AT THE COTTAGE DOOR'
is an example of one of Helen's earlier cottage studies executed before she settled in Surrey.

continue the freelance journalism he had taken up after he lost his post on *Fraser's*, receive visits from his friends and renew his acquaintance with George Eliot and her lover, who were spending the summer in their country house nearby. For the first time Helen painted outside, no matter what the weather. Her choice of subject reflected the influence of the Surrey countryside far more than Frederick Walker's and a recognizable Helen Allingham style was born.

It was the death of Carlyle in February 1881 which prompted the Allinghams to leave the capital and make a permanent home elsewhere. William felt the loss of his eighty-six-year-old friend and mentor so keenly that he could not bear to remain in Chelsea. When the search for a new home on the outskirts of London proved fruitless, Helen suggested they look in Surrey where they had spent several happy summers. Easily accessible from London by rail, the area around Haslemere was already popular with people like the artist Birket Foster, the publisher Edmund Evans and, of more significance to William, his hero the Poet Laureate. Although Tennyson retained his large house on the Isle of Wight, he had had Aldworth built as a summer retreat, complaining the island was being invaded by cockneys. In June 1881 the Allinghams and their two children decamped to a small hamlet called Sandhills near Witley in Surrey.

REFERENCES

1 William Allingham to Emily Lady Tennyson 10/8/74 (From the Tennyson Research Centre, Lincoln, by permission of Lincolnshire Library Service)

4
COUNTRY LIFE
1881–1888

The house that Helen moved to in June 1881 was ten years old, built of the traditional tile-clad red brick of Surrey cottages. It was no cottage, however, being the largest house in Sandhills. Confusingly the house was also called Sandhills since it abutted the sandy heathland which gave the area its name. Although Helen painted all the dwellings in the hamlet, some as many as six times from different angles, she only seems to have painted her own house once. As William Morris remarked soon after their arrival: 'Allingham's dwelling is a very pleasant and beautiful spot, but the house highly uninteresting though not specially hideous, nor the get up inside of it very pleasant (though not very bad), as you might imagine: the garden too is that discomforting sort of place that a new garden with no special natural gifts is apt to be. I should like to have made them better it.'[1]

Helen was unable to do much about the appearance of the house but she was intent on transforming the garden. She had inherited an interest in gardening from her mother but never before been given the chance to put her ideas into practice. Now, under the terms of the lease for Sandhills, there was a gardener's cottage and the services of John Hardy included with the property. Gradually Helen's ideas, drawn from the rambling cottage gardens she saw around her, and Mr Hardy's labour turned the large garden into a colourful array of old-

The only known painting of Helen's home Sandhills, executed in September 1881 soon after her arrival. William looks out of an upstairs window, while Gerald and Eva walk up the garden path. The present whereabouts of this painting are unknown.

'THE CATERPILLAR'
was painted during the 1880s in Surrey. Clematis montana, which rambles round the window, was a particular favourite with Helen and appears in other pictures.

A study of cottage plants, including roses, daisies and cornflowers, made in a Surrey garden and exhibited in 1886.

OPPOSITE:
This Sandhills cottage must have been one of Helen's favourites since she painted it at least eight times.

This cottage in Brook Lane was a short walk from the Allinghams' home and Helen painted it on three occasions from various angles. It appears in 'The Basket Woman' and 'The Elder Bush'.

'DIGGING POTATOES',
one of Helen's less idealized rural scenes.

fashioned plants like the wallflowers, roses, lilies and germander speedwell which can frequently be seen in her paintings.

There was no shortage of expert advice for interested horti-culturalists in the locality. Gertrude Jekyll, already known to William through a mutual friendship with the artist Barbara Bodichon, lived with her mother at Munstead House near Godalming. At this time Miss Jekyll regarded herself more as an artist than a garden designer. Nevertheless her opinions on the subject were sufficiently well regarded for her to be invited to judge at the Botanic Show (now the Chelsea Flower Show) in 1881. With a shared interest in painting and gardening, it was not surprising Gertrude and Helen should have become friends. Once Miss Jekyll had her own home and garden at Munstead Wood, Helen could often be found painting at the side of a flower border.

Tennyson, living just over the border in Sussex, was also a keen gardener and pleased to introduce the Allinghams to his friend James Mangles, a pioneer of rhododendron growing in England, who lived close to him at Valewood House. Once again the shared interest in gardening led to a lifelong friend-ship between Helen and the Mangles family. Over the years she painted their gardens, the cottages on their estate and portraits of children in their family. Even after she left Surrey, she regu-larly returned to the area on painting expeditions and stayed at Valewood House as a welcome friend.

The weather during Helen's first summer in Sandhills was glorious and she painted out of doors from the outset. Although her easel had been one of the first things to be unpacked on arrival, she rarely took it out of the studio. Frederick Walker had taught her to make do with knee, umbrella, or basket, indeed anything that was handy and required no fuss, to prop up her drawing board whilst working outside. Helen's choice of subjects reflected the inspiration she found in rural life: two women chatting over a wall, one feeding her hens, another pegging out washing, raking up the hay or baking bread. Nothing was considered too mundane to be painted and under Helen's brush even ordinary tasks took on a new beauty.

By the autumn of 1881 she was pregnant for the third time,

A superb example of Helen's cottage gardens, painted in such detail it is possible to identify every plant.

An especially fine Allingham painting entitled 'Over the Garden Wall', painted around 1880.

Valewood Farm which the Allinghams drove past regularly on their way to visit the Mangles family at Valewood House. Helen painted this lovely medieval house on many occasions.

'EVEY':
Helen's daughter, Eva Margaret, aged eight. Helen refused to paint portraits to order and, of the few she did execute, the best are of her own children.

OPPOSITE:
One of the very fine domestic scenes Helen painted showing her elder son Gerald and daughter Eva receiving lessons in the dining room at Sandhills

and the following May Henry William was born. Her elder son Gerald was then six and her daughter Evey five. Whilst Gerald delighted his father with the excellent progress he made with his lessons, there was concern about Evey. The pretty blonde little girl showed an interest in drawing but was slow to learn anything else. Gradually it dawned on Helen that her daughter was mentally retarded, something Helen found hard to accept and which eventually alienated her from the girl. By contrast, Henry, the only child to be conceived and born at Sandhills, received the full measure of Helen's maternal affection and became the symbol of the happiness she found in Surrey. Henry being cuddled by his nurse, fed, bathed and played with, was eagerly recorded by Helen's pencil in a succession of delightful sketches made just to please herself. The little boy with his fair curly hair was frequently dressed in pink frocks when he was young and appears, looking remarkably girl-like, in several of Helen's watercolours. From painting her baby, Helen went on to make more use of the older children as models in her pictures and began a series of charming domestic scenes in which they all appear. Frequently sketched in the dining room at Sandhills, the children can be seen looking at books, sitting at the table ready for a meal or learning their lessons with the governess. In outdoor scenes they appear blowing soap bubbles from a pipe, preparing a maypole or playing on the beach during a summer holiday.

In their early years at Sandhills Helen and William worked together on a book for the children called *Rhymes for the Young Folk*. It contained thirty short poems and songs written by William and was illustrated predominantly by Helen. Returning to her old skill of drawing on wood blocks, she portrayed the three children engaged in various gentle childhood activities and her husband sitting on the grass with Henry, introducing him to a leprechaun. A chance meeting with Helen's old friend Kate Greenaway, who regularly came down to Witley to stay with her publisher Edmund Evans and his family, led to the offer of two further pictures for the book from the country's leading children's book illustrator. Similarly an exchange of visits with another friend, Harry Furniss, an Irish cartoonist, produced two more line drawings for the book in a totally

It was uncommon for Helen to feature old people in her pictures,
particularly men. The child in pink is based on her son Henry.

OPPOSITE, LEFT:
The blond-haired Henry Allingham aged three, walking into a room
at Sandhills. In later life Henry was a car designer.

OPPOSITE, ABOVE RIGHT:
A sketch of Helen's favourite son Henry on a swing under the trees
at Sandhills; it was published as a book illustration.

OPPOSITE, BELOW RIGHT:
Drawings of Henry dominate Helen's illustrations in
Rhymes for the Young Folk.

different style. Caroline Paterson, Helen's sister, was invited to contribute some work which, along with two tiny sketches by William Allingham, made up the rest of the illustrations. The book was published in 1885 with the dedication: 'To Gerald, Eva and Little Henry, and others like them, this booklet is lovingly inscribed.' This remains the only example of Helen and William successfully combining their talents.

Occasionally Helen took a line from one of William's poems as the inspiration and title for a painting. 'When the grass is full of flowers, And the hedge is full of bowers' gave rise to a painting of a young girl laden with flowers, passing through a gate into a field full of ox-eye daisies, buttercups and harebells. The Allinghams made one other attempt to produce a joint piece of work but without commercial success. William wrote an historical play, *Ashby Manor*, which he tried to get taken up by one of the London theatre managers he knew. To assist the play's acceptance, Helen designed stage sets based on her knowledge of the theatre gained whilst on the *Graphic*. The interior of their house at Sandhills became the starting point for the set, disguised as a medieval hall, with its wooden panelling, large windows with window seats and gate-legged table recognizable in the pictures. Despite Helen's assistance, the play did

ABOVE:
One of several stage designs Helen made to accompany her husband's play Ashby Manor, *which was never produced. The sketches adapt features from the Allinghams' own home and from their wealthier Surrey neighbours' homes.*

OPPOSITE:
'BUBBLES'
was inspired by a visit to Tennyson's home in September 1884. To entertain his two grandsons, the poet fetched some soap and a pipe and proceeded to blow iridescent bubbles. 'Never was anything seen so beautiful,' he told Helen. 'You artists can't get such colours.' Helen rose to the challenge.

not find a producer. To the Allinghams' annoyance, however, a parody of *Ashby Manor* appeared on the London stage hammed up with plenty of melodrama.

This was only a temporary irritation and the years at Sandhills were some of the happiest and most prolific for William and Helen. No longer tied down by the deadlines of *Fraser's Magazine*, William was able to devote his time to writing poetry and contributing the occasional freelance article to periodicals. During the seven and a half years in Surrey he wrote and published at least one volume of poetry every two years.

Helen continued to paint and exhibited twice a year at the galleries of the Royal Society of Painters in Watercolours. Her pictures were frequently family scenes like 'Rock-a-bye Baby' which showed Henry with his nursemaid Elizabeth in the nursery at Sandhills, or studies of flowers flourishing in her garden or a neighbour's. A seaside holiday near Dover, where she saw a woman just returned from abroad, with her children in the charge of their Indian ayah, inspired several water-colours. More usually her pictures showed the inhabitants of Sandhills going about their daily life. Males rarely featured in Helen Allingham's paintings; it was the little girls and the young women pausing for a moment by their homes, who were most commonly depicted.

As time passed, the houses themselves engaged Helen's attention. Although the figures still held centre stage in her pictures, thatched and tiled cottages began to loom large. So popular did the cottages prove that the Fine Art Society in Bond Street invited Mrs Allingham to hold a one-woman exhi-bition of 'Surrey Cottages' in 1886. It was the Society's aim for the exhibition to show the countryside through four seasons, not easy for Helen to achieve when her pictures were invariably set in the late spring or summer. Ultimately, of the seventy pictures exhibited, thirty-seven were summer ones as against six winter ones. Even those six were mostly interiors, like 'Coming Events', which shows the living room of a cottage with an arm coming round the door, about to set a saucer of milk down for an eager cat.

The exhibition was hugely successful and so well reviewed

Unusual autumn tints appear in this cottage study. Autumn was not a season which normally inspired Helen.

OPPOSITE:
Helen's beloved son Henry being cradled by the children's nanny Elizabeth Haddon in the nursery at Sandhills.

ABOVE:
Helen was fascinated by this Indian lady and made many drawings of her which were used in other paintings. This scene is believed to be at Shanklin, Isle of Wight.

OPPOSITE:
In 1886 the Fine Art Society held an exhibition of Mrs Allingham's 'Surrey Cottages' portraying the seasonal aspects of the countryside. Vine Cottage was one of her summer choices.

A charming portrait of a young girl in a lilac sunbonnet. These bonnets were already out of fashion when Helen painted them but she kept her own stock of rustic costumes.

Helen called this portrait 'Kitty' which was her pet name for Félicie Keith, a child model who appears in many of Helen's later paintings.

OPPOSITE:
This picture, entitled 'Coming Events', was exhibited at the Fine Art Society in 1886 as one of Helen's winter scenes.

The only known self-portrait of Helen Allingham, painted in 1885 when she was thirty-seven.

OPPOSITE:
'THE CLOTHES LINE',
painted in 1879, employed the London model Mrs Stewart for the main figure. Ruskin criticized the picture for the coloured handkerchief which he said introduced a jarring note into the composition.

that the Fine Art Society offered Helen the chance of a further exhibition the following year. Although it meant a busy winter for her, selecting and preparing another eighty pictures, Helen was delighted to accept. 'In the Country', the title of the 1887 exhibition, gave her scope to display a wider range of subjects. In addition to studies of cottages and cottagers, she included a large number of flower studies and portraits of little girls with titles like 'Emmie', 'Tottie', 'Mary' and 'Nannie'. Ruskin, who had previously crossed swords with William Allingham on the subject of his wife's art, was quick to make known his dissatisfaction with Helen's portraiture: 'I am indeed sorrowfully compelled to express my regret that she should have spent unavailing pains in finishing single heads, which are at the best uninteresting miniatures, instead of fulfilling her true gift, and doing what the Lord made her for in representing the gesture, character, and humour of charming children in country landscapes.'[2] Helen was unrepentant. She had heard Ruskin pontificate on her work before and he frequently found something to criticize. The colour of a handkerchief in one picture was wrong; trees ought never to be depicted in full leaf; her skies were the wrong colour; she should not paint scenes in full sun. Ruskin might well be the doyen of the Victorian art world but, unlike Kate Greenaway, Helen was quite prepared to ignore him and paint what she wanted. *The Times* on the other hand was full of praise for her work, claiming it to be 'the very model of what an English water-colour should be'.[3]

In Surrey, Helen found a surprisingly good friend in Tennyson who, in his mid-seventies, was almost old enough to be her grandfather. William's friendship with the poet stretched back more than twenty years and was founded on a common interest in literature, but initially Tennyson had shown reluctance to meet Allingham's young wife. No invitation to visit the poet at his home on the Isle of Wight was issued, despite Allingham arranging holidays for Helen and the children at nearby Shanklin. Once the Allinghams were resident in Sandhills, six miles from Tennyson's summer residence on Blackdown ('further than we could wish', Allingham confided to a friend[4]), William was eager to establish an intimacy with his prestigious neighbour.

A portrait of Emily Lady Tennyson, wife of the Poet Laureate.

I made this sketch in 1887, I think, as Tennyson walked with my Husband up & down the Terrace at Aldworth, Blackdown, Haslemere.
Helen Allingham

Helen's experience as an illustrator and reporter on the Graphic *had taught her to record scenes quickly. This was necessary when Tennyson was the subject because he hated being drawn and would do his best to avoid it. Helen's own handwriting (above) records the occasion of this picture.*

At first Helen found Tennyson as crusty as Carlyle. When she sat down with her sketchpad, he became extremely agitated: 'You're staring at me – I can't bear it! He's keeping me in talk, it's a plot! I hate it! My back bone is weak! You mustn't, Mrs A,' he protested.[5] The painting came to nothing and only a pencil drawing survives. Helen did manage to snatch the opportunity to make an amusing little sketch of Tennyson pacing along the terrace at Aldworth, but it was several years later before she produced the fine watercolour portrait of the Poet Laureate reading in his study. The picture was never intended for exhibition, merely to be hung in Helen's home as a record of a friend. By this stage in her art career, Helen had little interest in producing portraits of great men and never attempted to paint Tennyson again.

At his request, she painted a portrait of Emily Lady Tennyson and one of his elderly dog Don, who in fact died the day after Helen finished the picture. Both portraits were treasured by the poet as were several small landscape scenes around Aldworth which Helen executed for him. She and Tennyson were enthusiastic walkers and would tramp miles over the Surrey and Sussex Downs in all weathers. This was not the sort of vigorous pursuit Lady Tennyson, who had become 'delicate' and taken to the chaise-longue, or William Allingham wished to participate in. Tennyson particularly enjoyed Helen's company because she too was interested in the countryside, yet quite prepared to walk along in silence contemplating the views and cottages in her own way without making any demands on him. Although Tennyson had been obstructive when Helen wanted to paint him, he did assist her in locating cottages and scenes worthy of portrayal.

Helen snatched this sketch of Tennyson during one of their first meetings. He became agitated: 'You're staring at me – I can't bear it! ... You mustn't Mrs A.' It was another ten years before he permitted her to paint his portrait.

'OLD DON',
Lord Tennyson's favourite dog, who accompanied his master on many walks over Blackdown. Helen painted this on 5 August 1880 during a visit to the Tennysons.

An outstanding portrait of Alfred Lord Tennyson in his study at Farringford painted in April 1890 with the poet's full cooperation. In earlier years he had tried his best to prevent Mrs Allingham drawing him.

'TENNYSON'S WOODS AT BLACKDOWN':
*I made this drawing in 1902, I think, looking southwards from Tennyson's Road
to his woods over Fox's Holes. The old road goes all the way through his property, skirting the garden
into a deep cutting called Packhorse Lane.*

A portrait of Rhoda Hardy, a local Surrey girl who later became Mrs Burgess, landlady of the Dog and Pheasant at Brook, near Sandhills.

'A SPRING GARDEN'
in a house close to Helen's own at Sandhills. It was the home of Mr Ayland, bellringer at Witley Church, and was always used for meetings of the Sunday School and Mother's Union before the village hall was built.

One amusing story of Tennyson's generosity to the Allinghams survives in the memoirs of the artist Harry Furniss who came over to Sandhills to view Helen's garden. She began by apologizing: 'It's somewhat untidy. Our garden implements and flower-pots and things are all over the place. Unfortunately our outhouse is taken up altogether with our White Elephant, and my husband cannot, of course, part with it, and we cannot use it.' The identity of the White Elephant was revealed when she opened the doors of the outhouse. It was a huge old-fashioned landau. 'We have no horses, but there it is – Tennyson's present to us, our White Elephant!' Helen explained with a laugh.[6]

William Morris said that in spite of its beauty, the Surrey and Sussex countryside did not quite touch him. 'For one thing it is very thinly inhabited, and looks more than most countrysides as if it were kept for the pleasure of the rich, as indeed it is,' he told Georgie Burne-Jones.[7] This comment certainly reflects Morris's socialist philosophy but also has some truth in it. According to James Mangles, Tennyson's gardener lived on the estate in a cottage which was in a dreadful state of dereliction. Because the house was covered in ivy, the great man claimed it was 'picturesque' and would have nothing done about it. Tennyson remarked to Helen one day when he was sitting watching her paint: 'Take a trim, snug, unbeautiful house, half ruin it, and you make it picturesque; same as ragged clothes.' William Allingham, who was also present, argued that neglect alone would not make a thing picturesque, it had to have beauty in it, but Tennyson was not to be drawn into an argument.[8]

Without doubt Helen idealized the countryside in her art, depicting a way of life which never really existed. The sun-bonnets on her models were freshly laundered props from the painting cupboard as women no longer wore them in real life. Much as Thomas Hardy did in his Wessex novels, Helen Allingham looked back nostalgically to a mythical pastoral age set sometime in the 1840s. The days were always sunny, the rosy-cheeked cottagers lived close to nature, did an honest day's labour and rested, well fed and content. Even in 1888 there were many who recognized that Helen Allingham's

Painted in the garden of one of the Allinghams' Surrey neighbours, this picture shows an older child than Helen usually depicted.

This Surrey farmhouse with its well and caged bird is not exactly as Helen saw it. The thatch and lattice windows had gone by then but she painted it as it could once have looked

In July 1885, William Allingham wrote to a friend: 'My wife is now engaged on a series of "Surrey Cottages" for exhibition by themselves next year in London and in this making record of many beautiful old things that are disappearing from the earth.' 'In a Witley Lane' was one of the pictures exhibited.

OPPOSITE:
Gertrude Jekyll and William Allingham were concerned about the preservation of this old cottage and a thatched one, both in Wormley Wood, Surrey. Sadly they were not able to prevent their demolition.

England did not represent the truth. The *Art Journal* in a lengthy article about her work stated that 'In Mrs Allingham's art there is no trace of sympathy with the stern realism to which we have grown accustomed in the works of many modern painters. For her there would be little attraction of a pictorial kind in the marks of grime and toil on rugged hands and bronzed faces... Still less is it Mrs Allingham's province to portray the sadder phases of child-life – the pale faces in crowded city streets, the boisterous and grim pleasures of such young urchins and romps.'[9] However, that the cottages around Sandhills with their uneven tiled roofs and flaking paint were inhospitable, even insanitary places at times, was well known to Helen.

Regular correspondence with Morris kept Allingham up to date with the progress of the Anti-Scrape Society, which campaigned to stop old buildings being irrevocably damaged in the name of 'restoration'. After a visit to St Albans with Helen to see her grandmother, Allingham communicated his concern about Gilbert Scott's 'renovation' of the church to his friend, urging him to attack the architect's work in detail. Morris was reluctant to fight Allingham's battles but sympathized with his complaint that a restored building no longer looked like an ancient one because its surface history had gone, and with it 'the venerableness of the sense of lapse of time'.[10]

Helen and William both felt strongly that the old cottages around them should be preserved from destruction or restoration. There is a curiously modern sound to Helen's complaint that all too often fine old building work, which had stood for years and was as firm as a rock, was replaced by cheap materials and careless workmanship in the name of progress. Old leaded lattice windows were ripped out to be replaced by 'modern' square ones of unseasoned wood while further up the road another landowner was having quaint 'old-fashioned cottages' with lattice windows built on his estate. In a strongly worded preface in the catalogue for Helen's 'Surrey Cottages' exhibition, William wrote that 'in the short time, to be counted by months, since these drawings were made, no few of the Surrey Cottages which they represent have been thoroughly "done up" and some of them swept away'.[11] The knowledge that

things were disappearing before her eyes spurred Helen on to record as much of old Surrey as she could. Alfred Tennyson and Gertrude Jekyll shared her concern and drew Helen's attention to threatened buildings. The inhabitants of course did not always understand what the artist was looking for and one well-meaning rustic, seeing Helen settling down to paint, advised her to return the following week, when 'there'll be a lot of new tiles and another coat of paint on this 'ere cottage'.[12]

The Allinghams' interest in preservation was not passive. In 1883 William organized a petition to prevent the absentee landlord, Lord Derby, who had recently purchased land near Hindhead, from enclosing it and barring access to the footpaths. Allingham took the petition round his influential neighbours like Lord Tennyson, Dr Tyndall the scientist, and numerous titled gentry. Following on from this he joined the

newly founded Haslemere Commons Preservation Society and published an article in the *Pall Mall Gazette* on the need to preserve footpaths. Although Helen did not actively campaign, her exhibitions of cottage paintings and the message in her catalogue did much to draw the subject to the attention of wealthy landowners.

William had taken Sandhills on a twenty-one-year lease but after only seven years he began to consider the advantages of the family returning to London to live. He was sixty-six and did not enjoy the best of health. Although he found greater pleasure in the Surrey countryside than he had thought possible, he nevertheless missed the life of the capital. Throughout their time in Surrey, he had been a frequent rail traveller up to London, often staying for several days at a time. With Gerald rising thirteen, William wanted to make better provision for his

A 1920s' photograph of the Allinghams' Surrey home taken when W Graham Robertson lived there. He maintained that the correct postal address for the property was 'Hell's Bottom, Lice Lane, Wormley, Surrey' but that none of the occupants would use it.

OPPOSITE:
Gerald Allingham, Helen's eldest child, painted in 1880 at Broadstairs, Kent. As an adult he became an engineer.

son's education than just the governess they employed in Surrey. Recalling Morris's condemnation of boarding schools after his time at Marlborough, Allingham felt strongly that Gerald must attend a day school and only University College School in Bloomsbury seemed to him to offer the appropriate education.

Helen's mother, brother Arthur and sister Carrie, as well as many intellectual friends, were living in Hampstead, so it seemed the obvious place for them to make their home. Word was put around that the Allinghams required a suitable house to lease and similarly that they had one on offer in Surrey. Several people came to look round Sandhills and eventually the house was taken by W Graham Robertson, the dilettante actor and artist, and his mother. William was delighted that someone theatrical was moving in and Helen consoled herself that Mrs

Robertson's interest in gardening would ensure her beloved garden did not go to rack and ruin. At the end of 1888 the Allinghams were able to move back to London.

REFERENCES

1 William Morris to Lady Georgiana Burne-Jones 23/8/82
2 *The Happy England of Helen Allingham* Marcus B Huish p83
3 Ibid p139
4 William Allingham to William Barnes 16/7/85
5 William Allingham's Diary 13/1/82
6 *Some Victorian Women; Good, Bad and Indifferent* Harry Furniss p80–1
7 William Morris to Lady Georgiana Burne-Jones 23/8/82
8 William Allingham's Diary 21/8/81
9 *Art Journal* 1888
10 William Morris to William Allingham 6/6/80
11 Fine Art Society catalogue 1886
12 *Art Journal* 1888

5

THE ESTABLISHED ARTIST
1889–1926

The Allinghams took a large house on the corner of Eldon Road in Hampstead, opposite their friends the Martineaus. Basil Martineau, son of the great Unitarian preacher and writer Dr James Martineau, was William's solicitor, and his wife Clara and sisters Edith and Gertrude were all artist friends of Helen's and lived in the same road. Nearby were Carlyle's niece Mary, by then married with a young family, Briton Riviere, the artist who had been so kind to Helen in her student days, and Kate Greenaway. Not only was Helen surrounded by friends, but most of her family lived in Hampstead as well and her uncle the Reverend Brooke Herford was minister at the Unitarian chapel in Rosslyn Hill.

The presence of so many friends and relatives was to be reassuring to Helen. A month before the move to London, William had consulted a doctor about his persistent indigestion. An enlarged gland was the diagnosis. But William suspected the worst, writing in his diary that he feared it was the first year of old age. In fact it was his only year of old age. His health deteriorated rapidly after his arrival in London and, though an operation in the spring brought temporary relief, he died on 18 November 1889.

In her mature paintings Helen frequently added doves to a roof to create interest at different levels.

At forty-one, Helen was a widow with three children aged fourteen, twelve and seven to support. Money had never been plentiful. After William had lost the editorship of *Fraser's Magazine*, they managed on various pensions he had, plus the income from his freelance journalism and the sale of Helen's pictures. At the time of his death William possessed only two hundred pounds to his name, so Helen knew she would have to work harder than ever at selling her work if the family were to survive. William's death naturally upset her deeply, although his twenty-five-year seniority and increasing frailty had prepared her for the parting.

Helen believed that her husband's work was superior to her own and she tried hard to gain for him the recognition she thought he was owed. In the years following his death, she rearranged, edited and published all his writings in an effort to keep his name alive. This work even extended to his personal diaries and letters. These were edited in a manner which would no doubt have pleased him: all personal or unflattering information was tactfully removed and much was made of Allingham's contacts with the rich and famous.

In 1891 Helen made her only visit to Ireland to see her husband's birthplace where his ashes rested. She took the children to the impressive monument that had been raised to their father by the side of the water of Ballyshannon Bay and to visit

It is rare to see shadows in an Allingham picture. This street is at East Hagbourne, Berkshire, and was painted during Helen's visits to her fellow artist Robert Anning Bell and his family.

This was painted in 1891 in Ireland, when Helen took the three children to Ballyshannon to see the birth and resting place of their father.

This picture and the one opposite are two different views of the same cottage at Pinner, Middlesex, painted in the 1890s. There is also a Kate Greenaway watercolour of this cottage in existence.

This cottage at Pinner, Middlesex, was painted in 1890 during a painting excursion with Kate Greenaway, who was supporting her friend in her recent bereavement.

the Irish relations they barely knew. In the weeks she stayed in Donegal, Helen painted around a dozen watercolours of the landscape and peasant cottages. The poverty and bleakness Helen saw in Irish country life rises to the surface in many of these pictures, in marked contrast to the mellow summers in her paintings of Surrey rural life.

As practical and resourceful as ever, Helen began on her return to restructure her life to ensure her children were cared for and her art could continue. One of her first acts was to engage a companion-cum-housekeeper, who could remain in charge at Eldon House while she was away painting or exhibiting. An unmarried genteel Scottish lady was taken on. In addition to her housekeeping skills, Miss Sarah Pirie was an accomplished pianist and made necklaces in her spare time for the new Liberty store.

Kate Greenaway proved a good friend to Helen in her early widowhood. Recalling that for years Helen had been urging her to try painting *en plein air*, Kate suggested they organize joint expeditions. She nominated Pinner in Middlesex as a suitable spot, being easily accessible by rail and containing many old cottages. They travelled there on numerous occasions and Helen successfully produced several pictures, but for Kate the experiment was a failure. Cottages were not her subject and her short-sightedness made painting out of doors difficult. 'What am I to do?' she asked Helen in despair. 'When I look at the roof it is all a red blur – when I put on my spectacles I see every crack in the tiles.'[1]

Believing the children's planned seaside holiday at Hastings would be more conducive to Kate's art, Helen invited her to join them. To her surprise the famous children's book illustra-

'AT SCHOOL GREEN, ISLE OF WIGHT'
was painted during a spring visit to the Tennysons in the early 1890s.

tor declined, saying that though she approved of the location and would have enjoyed Helen's company 'I should not be able to go ever if the children went.'[2] Kate did, however, agree to accompany Helen to the Isle of Wight when Helen was specially invited by Alfred Lord Tennyson.

On this her first visit to Farringford, Helen painted scenes of the poet's house, garden and views over Freshwater Bay, and in the hamlets around Freshwater she found many cottages to paint. Since Helen was as popular with Lady Tennyson and their son Hallam, much her own age, as with the poet, she was a welcome visitor and continued going to the area after Tennyson's death in 1892. Over the years she was to produce a large number of pictures of Tennyson's homes and favourite countryside. At the suggestion of Hallam, the second Lord Tennyson, she collaborated on a book, *The Homes of Tennyson* 'painted by Helen Allingham and written by Arthur Paterson' (her novelist brother), which was published in 1905 with twenty colour pages of her art.

The need for additional illustrations of the area around Aldworth obliged Helen to return to the borders of Surrey and Sussex. Although the area held many memories for her, they were happy ones and she was delighted to resume the friendship with Gertrude Jekyll, now in her own house, and with the Mangles family at Valewood. Despite Helen by then having a national reputation, with her pictures in demand for exhibition in the provinces as well as London, she nevertheless supported the new Haslemere Society of Artists and sent some of her paintings to their exhibitions until the end of the century.

Throughout the 1890s Helen worked at a prodigious rate, painting and exhibiting several hundred pictures. The cottage paintings were particularly popular and, with the need to earn her living, Helen continued producing such images. She did, however, experiment with other subjects. Living on the edge of London inspired her to paint a few urban scenes, and 'Stanfield House, High Street, Hampstead' is one of these unfamiliar Allingham pictures. There were one or two other smart town scenes, but Helen generally sought out a secluded Hampstead garden or one of the old cottages fast disappearing from the Heath to paint.

View over Freshwater Bay, Isle of Wight, painted during Helen's regular visits to the Tennysons in the 1890s.

*This timber-framed manor house was painted during one of Helen's
many excursions to Kent in the early 1900s.*

OPPOSITE:
*Stanfield House, Hampstead, in 1899 is a rare urban scene. Although
Helen painted several pictures of Hampstead, they were usually of the
gardens of friends or one of the cottages on the Heath.*

In search of fresh inspiration, she began to look at the Kent
countryside around Westerham. This was easily accessible by
rail from London and beginning to attract the attention of
various artists. Not happy in a large group, Helen ignored the
artistic gatherings and made her own arrangements to lodge in
a farmhouse on the Downs from which there were splendid
views. In the Kentish countryside, Helen painted not only the
humble cottages but also some of the grander manor houses.
Pure landscape, without figures or buildings, also suggested
itself to her. Many such pictures were harvest scenes emphasiz-
ing the contrast between the golden yellow of the newly mown
fields and the colours of the late-summer hedgerows. These
pictures tended to be for her own pleasure rather than sale.

In 1901 and 1902 Helen made a determined effort to
break away from rustic subjects. She paid two visits to Italy,
staying for some of the time with Gertrude Jekyll's married
sister, Caroline Eden, in Venice. Although Helen was in her
early fifties, the hundred or so paintings which resulted from
the Italian expeditions were radically different from anything
she had ever painted before. She took the opportunity to try
different light, subjects and perspectives. Several pictures
showed twilight or sunset and one, obviously influenced by the
Impressionists, depicted a night-sky shot through with starlight
and fireworks. The Venetian canals and boats delighted her, for
up until then Helen's opportunities to paint water had been
limited to a few seaside holidays and some village ponds. The
colourful street markets also resulted in several paintings.

On her return to England, Helen spent some time working
on the drawings she had made and by 1904 she was ready to
exhibit a large number of these new subjects. In her solo exhibition 'English Country Life and Venice' at the Fine Art
Society's galleries, Helen presented over sixty Italian pictures
but only forty English scenes. The exhibition was not a success.
The only Venetian pictures the public liked were those painted
in Mrs Eden's garden which, since the lady prided herself on
creating an English paradise, were indistinguishable from
scenes in a Surrey garden. Helen was disappointed but continued to exhibit the pictures for several more years hoping to
educate her public in this new departure.

Hardly a usual Allingham picture, this sunset was painted in Venice during Helen's expeditions of 1901 and 1902.

Helen at work in her studio. Her favourite painting chair appears in several interior pictures, was handed down the family, and is now preserved in the Hampstead Museum.

OPPOSITE:
'THE OLD BEECH TREE'
is one of Mrs Allingham's Kent pictures, though not a typical composition.

This typically English-looking garden picture has 'Venice' pencilled on the back and was probably painted in the garden of Mrs Eden (sister of Gertrude Jekyll), who lived and gardened there.

OPPOSITE:
'VENETIAN FRUIT STALL'
painted in 1902 was one of several pictures resulting from Helen's Italian holiday.

Retrieved from an Australian rubbish tip with a smashed frame, this Allingham painting has miraculously survived unscathed.

Her immediate election to full membership of the Royal Society of Watercolour Painters in 1890, the first woman to be accorded that honour, signalled the change in her fortunes and throughout that decade her reputation grew steadily. Despite the failure of the Italian pictures, Helen Allingham's fame and popularity were at their height around the turn of the century. She received regular requests for her pictures to go on exhibition in Europe and they were seen in Belgium, France, Italy, even Russia. At the 1897 Brussels Exhibition she was awarded the medal for watercolour painting.

By 1900 a typical Allingham cottage scene might sell for around fifty guineas and would be eagerly sought by many wealthy patrons. Ideally Helen herself liked to help a collector select a picture but that was not always possible since she spent an increasing amount of time away from home, painting. As her fame grew many art dealers and galleries wanted to buy pictures from her for their clients, and even the large London store Harrods was purchasing her pictures to sell.

So popular had Helen's work become that the art critic Marcus Huish proposed producing an illustrated biography. Initially Helen was reluctant. Being a very private person, she did not relish the publicity and was also uneasy about the reproduction of her paintings in a book. Colour printing was still in its infancy and Helen had seen the mess many printers made of reproducing watercolours. However, Huish was able to reassure her and *The Happy England of Helen Allingham* appeared in 1903, concentrating on her art rather than her life.

The commission to provide colour illustrations for a book called *The Cottage Homes of England* published in 1909 gave Helen great pleasure. This was dampened later by the realization that many of the books were bought by dealers just for the pictures to be split up, framed and sold. Helen had no objection to people having copies of her work on their walls, but she did object to dealers making large sums of money from such transactions whilst she earned nothing. Her younger son Henry, then in his late teens, tried to fight this injustice for her, but without success.

At the outbreak of the First World War Helen Allingham was sixty-six and continuing to paint in all weathers. The war

Pages from Helen's sketchbook, given to her grandson Patrick to paste in his album when he was a child.

The gardens of Manor Farm in Yorkshire show a more prosperous household than Helen usually portrayed.

Helen in later years. She continued her painting career until the end of her life.

frightened her and the news of an explosion in Holloway made her reluctant to stray far from Eldon House. Models were posed in her back garden or drawings made from old sketchbooks she had had years ago at Sandhills. Helen sent three or four paintings annually to the exhibitions of the Royal Watercolour Society during the period and until 1925, but there were no further large one-woman exhibitions of a hundred paintings as there had once been.

The First World War marked the end of Helen Allingham's popularity. Though she carried on working as hard as ever, in 1918 there was less interest in the work of a seventy-year-old lady whose style and subjects were old fashioned. That did not mean she considered retiring. Instead, Helen took on pupils. The late Vernon Ward recalled going for lessons at Mrs Allingham's studio at Eldon House, a room built on to the house by a former artistic inhabitant and irreverently known by the locals as 'the gun emplacement' since it jutted out and commanded a view up and down the road. Vernon was the son of Albert Ward, a Hampstead antique dealer and picture framer, to whom Mrs Allingham took her watercolours for framing, with the standard request for a three-inch gilt mount and a gilt-swept narrow frame. Mrs Allingham's idea of painting lessons for the young Vernon Ward and Meredith Frampton, son of the famous sculptor George Frampton, was to let the boys watch her paint and listen to her explanations. They were never permitted to put brush to paper themselves.

It was a disappointment to Helen that none of her own children wanted to follow artistic or literary careers. After school Gerald left home to take up engineering. He married twice and had one daughter, but maintained little contact with his mother. Helen, nevertheless, continued to keep him financially long after it was necessary. Evey's mental condition was a great tragedy and sometime early in the century, when in her mid-twenties, she was committed to an asylum. She outlived Helen but died hidden away, unknown and forgotten.

As in earlier times, the real light of Helen's life was her younger son Henry. Though he had no intention of becoming an artist or a poet, he was involved in early motorcar design, and his wife Nelly was the daughter of Royal Academician John

This white campion is the only known picture by Helen's daughter Eva. It was a present for Miss Pirie, the family's housekeeper-cum-companion and painted when Eva was eighteen. Although an amateur work, it is notable for her mother's influence.

'OUR PRIMROSE WOOD, BROOK, SURREY' was a gift from the artist to her son Gerald and his first wife Emily during the summer of 1913.

On the back of this picture Helen has written 'The Little Path, Kitchen Garden, Sharston Manor, Cheshire, 1920'.

OPPOSITE:
'VALEWOOD FARM'
from a slightly different angle from that in the picture on page 49.
This painting was bought directly from the artist by Birmingham Art Gallery in 1891 for fifty-five guineas.

Dated 1886 and inscribed 'To Alice', this portrait of Daphne Daffarn was a gift to her mother Alice (née Mangles) from the artist. The Daffarns lived at Valewood House where Helen was to spend her last few weeks.

Lomax. Helen doted on the couple and Nelly became the daughter she wished she had had. Their three children, Anthony, Patrick and Anne were much sketched as babies by their fond grandmother. In 1923, to Helen's intense pleasure, Henry agreed to bring his family to live with her at Eldon House.

In September 1926 Helen was once again visiting her beloved Surrey on a painting expedition and staying at Valewood House, still in the possession of the Mangles family but occupied by the married daughter Mrs Alice Daffarn. Despite having celebrated her seventy-eighth birthday on the twenty-sixth of the month, Helen was still sprightly enough to visit her old home Sandhills. With W Graham Robertson she strode over the heath and downlands she so much loved. But on 28 September she awoke in pain and died at Valewood House of acute peritonitis. Helen's estate amounted to a staggering £25,000 which kept her family for many years.

Like her husband, she had requested cremation. In Rosslyn Chapel, Hampstead, there is a memorial plaque to Helen Allingham, containing a quotation from Browning's poem 'Fra Lippo Lippi':

For, don't you mark, we're made so that we love
First when we see them painted, things we have passed
Perhaps a hundred times, nor cared to see;
And so they are better painted – better to us,
Which is the same thing. Art was given for that –
God uses us to help each other so
Lending our minds out.

REFERENCES

1 *The Life and Work of Kate Greenaway* M H Spielman and G S Layard p172
2 The Ivor Poole List of Manuscripts, University of Illinois

HELEN ALLINGHAM'S TECHNIQUE

Helen Allingham's pictures now receive greater recognition in the art world than at any time in the past. During her lifetime her popularity reached its zenith around 1900, but even then, because her work was in watercolour, it was considered secondary to that of oil painters. In addition her sex automatically placed her achievements below those of her male counterparts. Now that Helen Allingham's work can be considered purely on its merits, it is accepted as amongst the finest of nineteenth-century watercolours, with her cottage paintings second to none.

Her art is regarded as belonging to the Idyllist school whose members were watercolourists, heavily influenced by Frederick Walker, though seldom gathered into any formal groups. Like Helen, many had started their art careers as book illustrators and their work shows a common interest in the figurative subject and its relationship to the landscape. These artists frequently depict country subjects with a realism which permits the observer to believe, for a brief moment, that it is possible to enter their romantic world. Following Frederick Walker's lead, the artists went into the countryside to view rural life at first hand and to paint it *en plein air*. No activity was considered too humble for their brush. The figures appear to be caught for an instant as they go about their daily activities unaware of any intruder.

The accuracy with which she recorded the disappearing vernacular architecture has almost made her paintings into historical documents. Her cottages have the exact rows of tiles, with the patches of moss or unevenness present in the originals, yet sometimes they are not a true representation of what lay before her. She admitted that there was only one thatched cottage left in her part of Surrey by 1880 (that in Wormley Wood shown in her picture of the same name), but she depicted more. Those cottages which Helen believed had once possessed thatched roofs, she 're-thatched' in her paintings, using examples from her sketchbook drawn in Kent or Somerset. Similarly if she detected any evidence that a cottage had originally had diamond-lattice window panes, these would be 'restored' (she kept an old window frame in her studio to copy). Outbuildings, extensions and dormer windows also vanished as Helen sought to portray each as she thought it had once been.

The landscape around a cottage was treated with similar artistic licence. Most appear in isolation despite having close neighbours in reality. Features like church towers or other roofs which intruded into the skyline were removed, or masked by trees 'transplanted' from elsewhere to prevent the eye being distracted from the central subject. For the same reason Helen invariably used a high skyline and a somewhat plain sky of

FAR LEFT:
Although titled 'Under the Malthouse', it was not the actual malthouse which caught Helen's eye, but the doorway on the garden side. Birket Foster also painted this doorway but chose the view from the road. This picture was painted by Helen for exhibition in 1908.

LEFT:
The Old Malthouse as it appears today.

predominantly greyish tones applied as a wash pigment, then sucked back using a sponge or removed directly with a piece of rag. This earned her a grumble from Ruskin who wanted her to put blue skies into all her pictures: 'The devil sends grey skies,' he complained.

The glorious array of old-fashioned flowers which flourish in Helen Allingham's scenes again represent what she believed cottage gardens had once been like, rather than what she actually saw around her. Most Surrey cottagers planted up their plots with large quantities of vegetables to sustain their families through the winter; flower borders were a luxury. Some cabbage patches do appear in Helen's cottage paintings, but more usually her cottage gardens contain plants sketched in her own or Gertrude Jekyll's garden.

Unfinished pictures which survive show that Helen began work by painting the outlines of the scene on to her paper. This was done out of doors and with a brush loaded with a light blue or brown pigment rather than pencil or charcoal. The sky was then worked, followed by the trees and foliage. Although she painted quickly, as the vast number of her pictures demonstrate, Helen paid a great deal of attention to detail. Her trees and hedgerows for example are portrayed with a wide range of greens, mixed from a palette of nine or ten colours at most. In 1903 her paintbox contained cobalt, permanent yellow, aureolin, raw sienna, yellow ochre, cadmium, rose madder, light red and sepia; cerulean was added in 1911. From this somewhat restricted palette she created the different hues. To strengthen the darker colours she sometimes would wash over the dry

Since most of the original thatches had disappeared from Surrey by the 1880s, Helen had to travel to Somerset to make her drawings.

OVERLEAF:
This view of Hindhead, Surrey, was one familiar to Helen. It has an unusual perspective for an Allingham painting.

PAGE 101
Helen has captured the glories of a summer garden at Brook, Surrey, in such minute detail it is possible to identify every flower.

*Helen was always a keen observer of country life and noticed the sticks propped against the side
of the cottage which the man had collected to support his runner beans.*

OPPOSITE:
*The cabbages in this garden at Hambledon, Surrey, add a touch of realism to the idyllic scene.
The young boy was probably Helen's elder son Gerald and the baby her younger son Henry.*

painted surface with a solution of gum arabic so that a certain sheen is visible in these parts. Although much of her work was executed with fine brushes, she understandably selected larger ones when making broader statements and, on examination of certain areas such as the branches of trees, she appears to have used a hog's-hair brush. Another technique she favoured to give a greater illusion of texture to her work was to use the reverse end of a paint brush. By dragging the stick through the wet pigment she could not only disturb the surface of the paint but also physically impress the paper. Hedgerows and grassy areas in the foreground of her pictures can often be seen to be highlighted by such a method.

The point of focus in Helen's pictures is generally midground. Her foreground is slightly diffuse and leads the eye to the central area occupied by the cottage and figures. Thereafter the focus gradually diffuses again into the background. Her skill at handling this complex operation earned her unexpected praise from Ruskin. Comparing her work with that of her contemporary, Myles Birket Foster, Ruskin said that whereas Birket Foster painted everything as though it was under a magnifying glass, Mrs Allingham painted nature as it really was.

Once the landscape was complete, Helen turned her attention to the cottage. Although she is frequently referred to as a 'fair weather' artist painting only on sunny days in the late spring or summer, she actually worked out of doors all the year round and suffered from rheumatism in later years as a result. A letter written in 1900, when she was in her early sixties, commented that she was painting outside 'in spite of the snow'. However, only one snow scene exists, an 1870s picture. It would seem that in the winter months she concentrated on getting the architectural details of buildings correct, and if the weather became too wet for painting, she worked in the studio.

OPPOSITE:
This early Allingham farmyard scene uses Chinese White to create the white effect. It is unusual in having two boys as the main subject.

A rare study of an old lady. Grandmothers appear in the background of a few Allingham pictures.

It was here the figures and small animals were painted. Helen left blank spaces on the paper where features like these were to be put, and a close examination of a painting will usually reveal a faint 'halo' around such detail where her brush has been finely worked to merge the two areas into one. She rarely painted her figures out of doors, nor did she use local people as models. More commonly she employed a professional model and made large numbers of sketches at a time, posing the model either in her studio or in the garden. When the painting was brought into the studio for completion, Helen selected figures from her sketchbook to fill the spaces. It is for this reason that some faces and postures occur regularly in her pictures.

Young women and girls were her favourite figures but occasionally an old man or woman appears in the background. Boys were generally far too boisterous for an Allingham scene, so when seen they are usually lounging in the midday sun. An exception to this is her early painting 'Master Hardy's at Sandhills, Witley' where two children tug each other vigorously up a sandy bank above the Allinghams' house, much as Helen's own children would have done.

Animals regularly appear in her pictures but hardly ever as the main subject. There are birds on roofs, chicken on paths and cats creeping under hedgerows, included, she said, at her husband's suggestion, to provide interest and scale to the picture. Kittens, like young children, were her perennial favourite and popular with those who purchased her paintings, whereas larger animals like horses, cattle and dogs were rare.

The small details of faces, birds or flowers were added last. Incomplete Allingham pictures show that the artist applied the paint as dry as possible, building up the features gradually with small brush strokes. One child watching her work remarked: 'You do mess about a deal.' But the detail in the face of even the smallest Allingham figure is astonishing and can only be fully appreciated through a magnifying glass.

A technique which Helen employed increasingly after 1880 was that of scratching out. Until then she had sometimes employed Chinese White as a means of creating highlights. The pigment Chinese White was not easily available in England

Helen was fond of including small animals in her pictures, but this is one of the few studies of lop-eared rabbits.

OPPOSITE:
The sandhills which gave the area and the Allinghams' house their name. The cottage at the top was inhabited by John Hardy, the Allinghams' gardener, and his daughter-in-law Ada stands in front holding baby Ernest.

Helen made many studies of small birds and used these sketches to help complete her paintings.

This 1878 picture, painted during one of the Allinghams' summer holidays, uses Chinese White rather than scratching out to achieve the white areas.

OPPOSITE:
The farmyard scene is a rare Allingham subject depicting large animals; usually she portrayed only cats, rabbits and birds.

'COTTAGE AT ROUNDHURST'

with an excellent crop of ragwort in the foreground. Helen achieved her bold flower colours
by scratching back to the paper and flooding the area with pure pigment.

OPPOSITE:

This study of children at 'A Country House' was painted in the late 1870s when Helen was
using Chinese White rather than scratching out to achieve some of the white shades.

A page from Helen's 1870 sketchbook showing her interest in cottage interiors even when she was at art school.

An 1870 sketch of a cottage interior where the mantle ruffle is caught up in the same way as in 'Baking the Bread' opposite.

before 1834 when it was launched by Winsor and Newton's, but thereafter its uptake was rapid and it enjoyed great popularity. Respected critics like John Ruskin and artists such as Frederick Walker advocated its use but, as the century progressed, some watercolourists argued against it, saying that the opaque colours created when Chinese White was mixed with other pigments destroyed the essence of pure watercolour. Helen agreed with the move back to traditional watercolour techniques and the white which is seen in her pictures after 1880 is usually derived from the colour of the paper. Ducks, freshly laundered aprons or washing on the line in her pictures are often depicted by scratching out. Helen's essential tools when she was painting were her brush in her right hand and her 'pot scratcher', as she jokingly referred to her knife, in her left. She used the latter to striate the surface of the dry paint with tiny strokes to reveal the white paper beneath. The area was not always left white. Flowers in her paintings frequently reveal prior scratching out. After the foliage had been painted and when the pigment was dry, she applied her knife to the required tiny area then flooded it with pure pigment of a different shade to give a brilliant colour unadulterated by any previous underpainting. Birds on roofs, ducks in a lane or piles of logs in the foreground often show signs of scratching out, creating highlights and a greater illusion of texture.

When Helen considered her work finished she usually signed it at the bottom, either left or right, but she did not often date her work after 1880. One reason she gave for this was that though a picture might have been started very quickly it could be a long time before it was completed. Even without a date on a picture it is possible to work out approximately what period it belongs to because Helen Allingham's style, as well as her technique, changed over the years. Her earliest-known pictures are pencil sketches of her brothers and sisters, drawn when she was in her teens and living in Birmingham. From this

OPPOSITE:
'BAKING THE BREAD':
Helen has observed every detail of cottage life, even the flat iron stored alongside the main beam.

Again the Indian ayah appears with her charges in a seaside scene, this time 'On Dover Beach' in 1878. The picture is small, only four and a half by seven and a half inches.

time also is a watercolour of Kinmel Hall in North Wales painted when she was seventeen and on a family holiday in the area. The sketchbooks which survive from her days at the Royal Academy Schools are filled with figure drawings of fellow students which she used for her commercial illustrations. The sketchbook she took on her first trip to Italy in 1869 contains both pencil drawings and watercolours of the Italian countryside. Towards the end of this sketchbook are several well-executed pencil sketches of cottage interiors drawn at Limpsfield, Surrey, in 1870, which foreshadow her later pictures.

Not many watercolours signed Helen Paterson have survived, but the one of her sister Louisa, painted in 1871, is probably the finest. After her marriage Helen had more time to spend on painting and from 1874 onwards the number of paintings increases. From 1874 until 1881 when she moved to

Surrey, the influence of Frederick Walker is clearly visible in her work. These paintings frequently have a large central figure dominating the picture whilst the landscape is of less significance. Rural subjects fascinated her and during family holidays in Surrey she began sketches of women engaged in haymaking and similar occupations, which were worked up in her London studio. Many of her seaside scenes belong to the end of the 1870s when she took her young children to the Kentish coast. Early in the 1880s the family holidayed at Shanklin on the Isle of Wight and her other seaside studies, often depicting the Allingham children playing on the beach, were executed then.

It is the move to Sandhills in 1881 which marked the turning point in her art. Helen rejected the use of bodycolour (the mixing of Chinese White with other watercolours to achieve greater opacity) and at the same time became interested in the relationship between figures and their backgrounds. She

One of Helen Allingham's small number of seaside studies, painted during family holidays at Broadstairs, Kent, in the late 1870s.

This cottage with its glorious display of climbing nasturtiums was adjacent to the Allinghams' own home at Sandhills and was painted on numerous occasions by Helen.

OPPOSITE:
The hen with her brood of chicks has caught the attention of the young girl in this charming spring scene.

The little girl cradles her doll outside a thatched cottage near Crewkerne in Somerset.

was highly critical of her early pictures, saying the figures looked too much like studio models superimposed on a landscape. Her single central figure gave way to several figures who appear more concerned with their own activity than in posing for the onlooker. Young children began to feature regularly in Helen's pictures as did rural themes like feeding the chickens or watching a pedlar. The figures diminished in size and the landscape gained in importance and detail.

Helen began painting cottages during her years at Sandhills, but the scenes most readily associated with her belong to the 1890s when she had returned to London. By then the figures in her pictures were small and an integral part of the landscape. Helen said she had decided it was possible to put as much of interest in a tiny figure as in a large one. A little girl cradling a doll or a mother holding an infant appears in many such paintings but they do not detain the eye. Indeed in a few pictures there are no figures at all. To her way of thinking the cottage was the central feature, and she viewed it in the same way as other artists did a portrait. Her paintings show the character of the buildings, with their lines of age and neglect.

At the end of the 1890s and into the twentieth century, Helen Allingham was moving towards landscape painting. Her downland and harvest scenes around Westerham in Kent, where she went on painting expeditions, often included no figures, but never sold as well as the cottage scenes complete with young children and kittens, so Helen had to continue painting variations on that theme for the rest of her life. The Venetian pictures of 1901 and 1902 and the few French drawings executed *en route* remain isolated examples of the way her art might have developed if she had been financially independent.

Portraits she painted throughout her life but in small numbers. Her pictures of Thomas Carlyle, Alfred Lord Tennyson and William Allingham testify that she was

OPPOSITE:
'THE FIDDLER',
exhibited in 1886, is one of the few paintings Helen did with a man as the main figure.

A study of Aitre, St Maclou, in Rouen made in the early 1900s when Helen was travelling to Venice.

OPPOSITE:
'HARVEST FIELDS AT WESTERHAM' is one of Helen's later landscapes. These pictures without figures were never popular with the public.

exceptionally good at this art form despite having no desire to develop it. She was frequently asked to paint people's children but usually declined, saying that she thought portrait work too restricting. Those Allingham portraits which exist are either of her own family or were painted as presents for friends. They, along with the wide range of other subjects, show the outstanding talent of Helen Allingham.

CAROLINE PATERSON SHARPE

Interest has steadily increased in paintings by Helen Allingham's sister. Caroline Paterson (1856–1911) received art training in London and followed in her sister's footsteps as a book illustrator. She painted in watercolour employing similar techniques to her sister which makes it easy to confuse some of her family portraits with the work of Helen. Caroline Paterson's pictures typically depict one or two children as the central figures and are of a more sentimental nature than her sister's. Interestingly, the Allingham children appear as models on occasions and the interior of Sandhills is also recognizable in the background of a few of the pictures. She continued painting after her marriage in 1894 to Sutton Sharpe and some landscapes date from this period. Caroline Paterson's work however never enjoyed the same success as Helen Allingham's.

ABOVE:
'CAT'S CRADLE'
is the work of Helen's sister, Caroline Paterson, who followed Helen to
art school and into book illustration, but never achieved the same fame
as a professional artist.

OPPOSITE:
Thought by many to be the finest example of Helen Allingham's art,
this picture shows her daughter Eva giving the youngest member of the
family his first reading lesson.

BIBLIOGRAPHY

Allingham, Helen and Baumer Williams, Mrs E (ed) *Letters to William Allingham* (Longman 1911)

Allingham, William *Rhymes for the Young Folk* (Cassell 1885)

Baldry, A L *The Practice of Watercolour Painting* (1911)

Chapple, J A and Pollard, A (ed) *The Letters of Mrs Gaskell* (Manchester University Press 1974)

Clayton, Ellen *English Female Artists* Vol 2 (1876)

Dick, Stewart *The Cottage Homes of England* illustrated by Helen Allingham (Edward Arnold 1909)

Furniss, Harry *Some Victorian Women; Good, Bad and Indifferent* (John Lane, The Bodley Head 1923)

Grigson, G (ed) *Diary of William Allingham* 2nd Ed (Centaur Press 1967)

Huish, Marcus B *The Happy England of Helen Allingham* (A and C Black 1903)

Knies, Earl (ed) *Tennyson at Aldworth: The Diary of James Mangles* (Ohio University Press 1984)

Leslie, G D *The Inner Circle of the Royal Academy* (John Murray 1914)

Lester, Anthony *The Exhibited Works of Helen Allingham* (The Lester Gallery 1979)

Mackenzie, Tessa (ed) *The Art Schools of London* (Swan Sonnenschen 1896)

Paterson, Arthur *The Homes of Tennyson* with twenty illustrations by Helen Allingham (A and C Black 1905)

Robertson, W Graham *Time Was* (Hamish Hamilton 1931)

Spielman, M H and Layard, G S *The Life and Work of Kate Greenaway* (A and C Black 1905)

Stirling, A M W *William De Morgan and his Wife* (Thornton Butterworth 1922)

White, Gleeson *English Illustration "The Sixties"* (Constable 1906)

INDEX